Thomas Townsley

Tangent of Ardency

SurVision Books

First published in 2020 by
SurVision Books
Dublin, Ireland
Reggio di Calabria, Italy
www.survisionmagazine.com

Cover image: *S* by John Chamberlain; the Hirshhorn Museum and Sculpture Garden, Washington, DC

Design © SurVision Books, 2020

ISBN: 978-1-912963-14-0

Acknowledgments

Grateful acknowledgment is made to the editors of the following, in which some of these poems, or versions of them, originally appeared:

SurVision: "A Month of Thursdays," "Tangent of Ardency," and "Accordion-Playing Clam"

Contents

A Month of Thursdays

A month of Thursdays I waited, nibbled by hedge hogs
of regret. A month of Thursdays, my eyes gouged
by real crows who spoke to me so I would not
feel alone; they said "This is the whitening, the
cleansing of matter." "Then why is it so dark?"
I asked, for I had no understanding. A month
of Thursdays, a cyclops's eye. A month of Thursdays,
a razor blade's reminiscences, an eel's sense of purpose,
a hot pavement strewn with starfish like cookies on a tray.
The turning wheel evokes a sound of bells. A month of
Thursdays, and no mention of the diadem. Does the night
have teeth? Are there voices in the well? I'm clutching
father's war medals, through which the radio signals come.
A month of Thursdays, time's barbed wire around my throat,
lungs turned to pumice. "We've brought you company,"
say the crows. "His name is Paracelsus. He will explain
everything." But all he does is spit in my ear. This restores my
vision, but it's not the same because the memory of
darkness overlays everything, save that which is holy,
and there's nothing I can do about it.

Tangent of Ardency

Beside a house with liver spots,
near the coughing lilacs, flows a brook
that turns the calendar's pages and
bears away flotsam shaped
like tiny hats.

"Where are the lovers?" it seems to ask.

In the wooded glen nearby, the lovers crouch
amidst allegorical figures who declare
their relationship to Fate, using the
language of antiquity.

The lovers are ignorant of this language.
Beside them bubbles a spring, the brook's source,
with its tale of loaves and fishes,
of many from one.

From here, one can see pinecones dropping.
One can dine on the meat of the sky,
which replenishes itself like
tankards of ale for rich men.

From here, one cannot see the obsidian threads,
nor feel the disbursements. One cannot taste
the imploding compass. Here, it is said,
one never waits but always remains.

Accordion-Playing Clam

To make a clam play an accordion is to invent—not to discover.
—Wallace Stevens

What are the parts of a pier? Planks and pilings?
Shall I risk my life for a poem? My dog eats snow
and leaves his water bowl untended. How then
shall I weigh shame? By the clam's beard I'll know thee,
by its "Lady of Spain" I'll measure this song,
though seabirds lack color and the waves' paraphrase
misquotes, endlessly misquotes, things as they are.
Once, I lived with gypsies; they gave me a secret name
without purpose, like a rosary seen through a crystal ball,
like invisible cuff-links. I use an adder's fang
for a hat-pin, for all the good it does.
Refrigerators humming Mozart, cotton fields of
white regret, the *e pluribus Unum* of doorbells in childhood,
arcane musings of Egyptologists at the Fratricide symposium—
these and more shall grace thy song.
What are the parts of reality, that they might
be discovered at a Sunday morning's tea or at this clam recital?
The most colorful birds dwell inland, along emerald rivers.
Their drowsy songs breathe false fire; though it light
a thousand nights, it will not burn.

Tuesday

What can be said of Tuesday that Neruda hasn't said—that old perfusionist of dreams? Is it a day for counting blessings? Very well. I have a wound for each finger of my left hand, plus a scar shaped like a capital I. My convalescence is spinning off the rails. My beard sprouts dandelions. There's a howling wilderness in my spleen. My friends say I'm recovering nicely, but a flock of cormorants has settled in my lungs, and my kidneys whistle "Sewanee River" in the dark. A rehearsal of "Titus Andronicus" is commencing in my bowels. Thank goodness for the exegetes in white, who visit me and dispense their aphorisms whenever time begins to unknot. "Remember, an ending is just a snake's tail in the mouth of a beginning," they say, and "Things seen in retrospect can't be trusted." But isn't everything seen in retrospect? I wonder. Of course, they never answer because they never stay that long, leaving me to my Tuesdays and this string of antitheses. Ah, Tuesday, with its handprints on the mirror, its leftover apple sauce, and its bitter albumen. Is it not in memory that the world's inscriptions become legible? Who will wash me in a spray of hesitancy and gild these doubts? I look to God, who extends a bony finger and pokes me in the eye; what that eye sees is now unhinged from time and space, which were never properties of this world but of our blindness. My other eye is bitter. It is tired of living in foxholes. "Who needs all this marginalia?" it seems to say. I share its agitation, but the terraced light of a March afternoon has a welcome placebo effect, forestalling the apocalypse and brushing hair from the doily. Don't ask me what that means, but it wouldn't be Tuesday without it—Tuesday of Hair and Doilies, Tuesday of Reticent Carbuncles, Tuesday of a Bigamist's Cologne, Tuesday of a Sundering's Aftertaste, Tuesday of Laughing Nerudas. What we need is a conflagration, or at least a star to steer by. I'm tired of songs of umbrage. There was a time these stuttering hands invented a lover's

8

body, and my tongue proclaimed it a world. The nick of time was a gaping wound we played in. Now it's Tuesday of the Rattling Spine, and I dream about vaudeville and soft shoe routines. My thyroid longs to be governed by the moon. Perhaps a good housecleaning would help. I look around this dusty living room, and I remember what Great Grandma Martin used to say—well, no, I don't. She died before I was born, but I'm told she said this to her daughters as she handed them their dustpans and brooms: "Clean the corners, girls, and the rest will take care of itself."

The Surrealist's Rose

Borne across serpentine dunes by a caravan of fire ants,
The blood-dripping rose   Bitter vortex

Borne to the edge of a scabrous sea, too salty for dreams,
Rose of holy fire   Map of time's fugue

The sea extends a foaming finger and touches you.
It touches petal and thorn.

At once it ceases mirror-making.
The stars retract their needles of light.
The moon, so lonely it would die for a single petal's caress,
Withdraws its reflection forever.

Hieratic rose   Death's doorbell

Selective Amnesia at the Convalescents' Ball

Someone in steerage is juggling compasses and whistling sad circus tunes. "I never understood chandeliers," he says.

Just then, a busload of Fauves pulls up to the sanatorium. From our dark rooms, we listen to the bustle they're making in the lobby: clattering easels, accordion music. Are they checking in? They are! Hide your vermilion!

A man with a face so dog-eared it can't be seen takes everybody's blood pressure.

I enter the ball room. It looks like an ordinary living room, except for the frescos depicting executions of religious heretics.

A woman in a sequined dress floats toward me—the hostess? "Friedrich!" she says. "Friedrich, darling! I'm so glad you could come."

"My name's not Friedrich," I tell her, but by then she has brandished a syringe and plunged it into my neck. "What's that for?" I ask.

"Why, the pain, of course," she says. "What else?"

I am losing control of my memory.

Is it true that any observation creates its own relevant history?

My eyelids are made of glass. Therefore, closing them is pointless.

A new arrival—a young man with dark hair that curls about the ears—realizes to his chagrin that no one else is wearing a surgical mask.

"You'll have to dream harder," the sequined woman tells him, "if you want to taste the big hors de oeuvres."

Meanwhile, someone in the hold is screaming in a shrill falsetto: "Borneo jelly! Borneo jelly!" At least that's what it sounds like.

Could it be some of the Fauves have gone over to Dada? Has their ban on earth-tones worn thin?

The best ploy is to keep quiet, seem indifferent, and let time do its work.

Someone fires up the old Victrola. I know I've heard the tune before. I think it was *our song*, but I can't remember the name. It sounds like it's playing underwater.

Wait!—*our song?* Is this ball being thrown in your honor? Is it your portrait the Fauves have been painting all along?

The chandelier makes a sound like bells. The memories return, washing over me like a flood. Am I becoming whole? Or am I drowning?

This epiphany is interrupted by the new arrival, who sidles up to me and whispers, "Say, old chap—what on earth is Borneo jelly?"

"Go away!" I tell him. "I'm contemplating my second person pronoun! I'm recovering my personal history."

"You seem upset," he says. He takes hold of my wrist. "Let me check your pulse."

"I'm warning you! Someone in my head wrote this poem for you to bleed on," I tell him.

"Relax," he says, smiling. "It looks like you've done enough bleeding for both of us."

Sooner or Later, a Title Will Occur

You go so far, and then you pull back.

Your thoughts have grown hard as a nautilus shell.

Everything spirals in the same direction, down to the same point.

You see a woman named Ada in a feather boa, or read about a claims adjuster with dirty secrets.

Maybe a petulant obfuscator has hazelnuts for lunch.

Are these signs of bigger signs to come?

Stuck in traffic for hours in an un-air-conditioned bus, a mime troupe gives vent to its rage.

An ex-lover calls to say scientists have discovered a new constellation shaped like regret.

Walking past the orphanage at 3 am, you hear the faint whine of power tools.

You want to bring it all back to pie-eyed angels, to mirrors and swans.

You wish to ponder semi-precious stones and ideas that begin with capital letters. Instead, you get an old woman selling pink hats for snakes.

You begin to write dramatic monologues that take the form of limericks.

An ex-lover calls and says she'd like to meet you. You follow the GPS to the address she gave, and find yourself in a Roman coliseum. When the iron gate behind you opens, the entire crowd says "Uh oh" in unison.

Where are the long jetties and mist-shrouded piers?

Why does the lake sound like a roomful of children eating crackers?

An administrator paces in front of the Savings & Loan, wearing a placard that says "Inscape."

The bell rings. Three Presbyterians stand at your front door, selling timeshares. "Forsake your whelk-love," they say. They don't know you keep a clerical collar hidden beneath your turtleneck and carry cardboard moons in your hip pocket.

A grocer with a moustache and a bad conscience sits on a porch swing, listening to the white noise of cicadas. "Some people always talk with their triggers pulled," he says.

You've got a horizon full of broken statuary where the allegories used to be.

An ex-lover calls. She seems nostalgic. "I remember the last time I saw you," she says. "It was at the train station. You were waving from the passenger car window, wearing that mauve sweater your mother gave you. You seemed both sad and exhilarated. Then you shouted 'We'll always have Cedar Rapids!' as the train pulled away."

Of course, you've never been to Cedar Rapids, but you remember it like it was yesterday.

The Festival

Gimcrack sunsets, ice cream trucks playing Hindemith,
paucities of hummingbirds.

Have you been measured for the festival?

When I was a child, I put away
my rusty egg-beater. Still, I felt no different.

Invisible bread waiting for its cue to fall from the sky,
a preponderance of shovel-leaning,
a box full of extended warranties.

I am a big, big man.
They say I am a big, big man.

The shed is white; the last hummingbird lives inside.
I hid in the closet beneath the stairs.
I was not ready for atonal ice cream.

Have you been measured for the festival?

Genetically mutated alfalfa, thyroids run amok,
everything made from molasses.

They say my dreams are real, but I don't
know what that means.

There are twelve notes in the chromatic scale.

Bowing impresarios in red jackets, death penalties
for U-turns, sapphires stashed in flower pots.

May I wake up now, please?

Mr. Hummingbird says it's not polite to stare.
But I can't help it.

The festival is almost here,
and I think I'm bigger than you.

Call It "Untitled" Then

At the narrator's departure, the mirror dreams of its own light.
Stray images swarm around the sleeper's head:
bittersweet vines climb into the reddening twilight,
a congregation is tormented by mosquitos,
someone sets the hymnals on fire,
someone distributes the sacrament in silver thimbles.
Is it time to empty your eyes?
"Alas," says the former narrator, "I'm just another Cassandra,
spilling the wine."
And so, the present bursts upon us.
Night confers its fears. The distempered metronome
trembles in the dark. "Is this still a fiction?" asks the reader
suffering from aspect-blindness.
And the ocean turns its unread pages.

Maintenance Required

Why can't you write nice poems about blackberries? Or should I say "Wherefore"? Instead, these indicator lights keep coming on, and we've barely set out. Oh please, not another journey poem—or worse, a quest. "What vision do you seek?" asks Iron John, and now everything's shot to hell.

August refuses to get out of bed. The birds sashay in the all-knowing linden tree. *Looks like a problem with the differential. That'll cost you.*

Hey, check it out! See how ragged robin covers the neighbor's field like eczema? I told you we barely set out! A pall of belatedness settles over everything—even "nature," as depicted on these place mats. "There's nothing left to defamiliarize," says Iron John, "so let's make s'mores. Do you grow your own kale?"

Metal filings in the transmission fluid—not good.

"I drove for a year with the Check Engine light on," you tell me. "Never had a problem." It depends on what you mean by "problem," I suppose. Remember how you looked for acrostics in your alphabet soup? These are the days between parentheses, where comma-filled afternoons trail off in ellipses... Well, I say "Once more to the lake!" I'm bringing the pop-up. And see? We've already made it to the woods or the mountains or whatever. That didn't take long, oddly enough. Now something's rattling under the hood. Let's pull over and take a look. Maybe that man with the boar's tusks can help us.

Night of Yellow Frogs

The tattooed woman who lives in the wall tells me to confess. I can deal with her later. She's just one of many distractions.

For instance, someone has poured more water than I care to admit in my shoes—I'm sure there's a French phrase that describes it perfectly—but I must continue apace, painting Mother's ceramic eggs black. I've been at it for what seems like days. Mother was quite a collector! Her eggs fill thirteen rooms, each with a view of the moon, whose phases vary, depending on which room I'm in. Each individual egg is painted with its own unique design. Or was. I'm working at a feverish pace, using a condor feather dipped in the darkest ink. I found that a flat black covers the surface with only one coat, and so my mountain of black eggs grows quickly—their exquisite details eclipsed forever: "Goodbye, hyacinths," "goodbye stars," "goodbye unicorns," "goodbye, maidens beneath the willows." Still, when I confront what remains to be done, *je suis attere' par l'ampleur*—I'm overwhelmed by the magnitude of the task.

And then there's the incessant mockery of the yellow frogs, who saturate the night with their croaks and whispers, their malignant innuendos. They are the worst distraction of all. Where do they come from? How did they get here—and in such noisy abundance? I'm convinced they've climbed the swamp's one great tree in order to project their barbaric suggestions directly through my window. *"Petits vers de morve!"* I shout." Little snot worms! When I'm through with these eggs, you're next!" But they pay no heed, as is the way of yellow frogs. Don't they know my supply of ink is endless? No, their silky alarums persist—if anything, they grow louder, until I feel they are suffusing my skin, until I feel tadpoles infiltrating my bloodstream, until I am myself a teeming swamp whose many vapors bedizen the stars with gauze.

When their cacophony becomes intolerable, as inevitably it must for a man of my age and working habits, I throw the condor feather to the floor and cry out, *"Le urgencies amphibies, me laissant a` mon travail!"* But I am already wet to the knees. I slosh over to the window and draw the shades against a pernicious gibbous moon. Still their insidious frog music persists, each peep a yellow hole in the silence I crave, so I press my hands to my ears, and I back up to the wall, screaming *"Petits vers de morve!* I haven't time for this! Leave an old man to his obfuscations!"

And then, as if spurred by my cries, two slender, tattooed arms reach out from the wall and clasp me tightly about the waist. "Now I have you!" she says. Judging from her tone of voice, I know it's useless to struggle. "All right!" I say. "You have me! What is it you want me to confess? Tell me now, and let's be done with it!" She makes no answer but begins to draw me towards her. My back is pressed tightly against the wall, but I feel my resistance ebbing. I have just enough time to observe the tattoos, a pattern of alternating letters and skulls, each ablaze in a row of feathery green flames that span the length of her forearms. "Funny that I never took the time to notice these until now," I think to myself—and that's my last thought before she pulls me inside.

The New Albanian Novel

Typically, the crepuscular light emanating from the heroine's wardrobe must be implied or acknowledged through an idiot's monologue, but the good news is our mice look healthier than ever. What a sheen! Their coats sparkle like bad ideas. It's mid-October. The famine's been cancelled. A starling's warbling song sounds vaguely autobiographical, and is an essential ingredient of a healthy breakfast. I am rearranging my files perpendicularly, so that they feel less antediluvian. The "de-centered subject" is a standard protagonist in the New Albanian Novel, like crows on a clothesline, each with its own ideological poo poo platter. Multiple points of view may be further divided—"a potato for every orphan," as they say in The City of Parallelograms. Have you seen our Festival of Purple Lights? It's a holiday invented by the government to remind us of our civic responsibilities, financial and corporeal, with accompanying musical jingles to sear them into our brains. The New Albanian Novel must sweat multivalent spiders out of us, using the power of broken syntax, a stiff-lipped rejection of hermeneutical flourishes, and words that stick like burrs. The new condominiums produce people of vast neutrality; all of their beach towels are white. Albanians! Do you see that cloud? Why is it mediocre? Why is it always accordion music and hats with feathers? Does our largesse as a nation make up for our neglect of the classics? Why can no one read the New Albanian novel, much less write it? Is it because all of our artists are still painting shoes? Who will capture the gray egg yolk of our dawns, our flatulence and rust, in prose or verse? What are these burrowing insects with seven legs that feed upon our radishes? Why are the lighthouses out of order? When will our dwelling places no longer resemble rows of bad teeth? New Albanian Novel, we wait for you, your gruel of sympathy, your comic theology dangling on a hook, and your puzzling opacities which always invite the landfill of critical essays to follow.

The Shampoo

The fog rolled out and took us with it. In the mist,
I heard Mrs. Dewdrop complaining that her bedsheets'
thread count was below average. "Just like your children's IQs,"
someone said. "Who is that?" Mrs. Dewdrop shouted.
"I dare you to come here and say that to my face." But whoever it
was stayed hidden in the fog. By this time, our feet left the ground,
lifted by a tide of vapors; it was like being imprisoned in a
giant marshmallow floating out to sea. Or something like that
I heard laughter off to my left. Was that Father Flanagan?
"Only venal sins," he was saying. "Only venal." Then his laughter
became maniacal. I couldn't tell if I was upside down or
right side up. "Arms akimbo!" cried a voice that sounded like
Officer Carruthers. "It's important to maintain balance. Remember
Vitruvian Man, the circle and the square," he said. Someone
screamed from the mist, "Only an idiot would revert to classical form
at a time like this." "Who said that?" barked Officer Carruthers.
"Don't think I won't arrest you." "Why don't you cartwheel over here
and try it, Vitruvian Man?" said the voice. *People are braver in the
fog*, I thought. I drifted on and on. I heard clocks chiming, babies
crying, dogs barking. I heard young lovers telling lies. After a while,
I heard the sound of water. Through the fog, I could barely make out
the form of our Leader, sitting in a bath tub. "Who's there?" he
shouted. "Nobody," I said. "Are you my shampooer?" he asked. "No,
I'm not your shampooer," I said. "Why not?" he snarled. "I don't
know," I said, "but I'm not." "Then where is he?" The Leader
demanded petulantly. "He was supposed to be here at six." "Maybe
he got lost in the fog," I said. "I didn't order any fog," The Leader
replied. "That may be, but as you can see, it's here," I said. "And so
are you," The Leader said. "Now get over here and shampoo me.

That's an order." "I would," I said, "but the problem is, I have no hands. I lost them in a childhood accident. All I have are these very sharp hooks." "Liar!" shouted the Mystery Voice. "Hear that? You're lying," The Leader said. "No one has hooks anymore—unless you're a pirate. Are you a pirate?" "No, I'm not a pirate," I said. "That's good. You wouldn't want to see what we do to pirates. Now no more excuses. I want my shampoo. Shampoo me, or it's curtains for you! You don't even want to know what awaits prisoners in the State dungeon." "There's a lot I don't want to know," I said, pouring a dollop of shampoo on my hand. I rubbed my palms together and worked up a good lather. Then I began to massage it into his scalp. "You got that right," said The Leader. "There's a lot I don't want to know, either. But I have to. It isn't easy." "I'm sure it isn't," I said. "Have you ever thought about retiring?" "I have," he said. "I've dreamt of having my own horse ranch in the mountains. I'd have an aviary there, too." "That sounds nice," I said, trying not to notice the strange bumps on his scalp. "Why don't you give up all this responsibility and do that?" "I have too many enemies," he said. "They'd kill me the second I relinquished power. I'm afraid that the ranch, the retirement—all of it—is just a dream." "That's too bad," I said. "It must be difficult, being in your position. I feel sorry for you. And I'm sorry that I made up that business about the hooks." "Don't worry about it," The Leader said. "Happens all the time. But if you get any soap in my eye, I'll show you what burning feels like. Do you understand?" "I understand," I said.

Incubator

Time for a little reading, maybe? Not the deeply analytical,
competitive reading one poet gives another, nor the page-
turning anticipation of novel-lovers. Instead, just a few words
to make you scratch your head, look over your shoulder,
as if a door is opening behind you; you hear something wet
and slithery, or perhaps a band is playing oompah music;
you remember something someone said thirty-seven years ago
that made you sad; all the while, the weatherman is calling for
peccadillos; you feel the need to look up "trivet," and by this time a
few of your mother's hummels are begging you for a sip of whiskey;
in the guest bedroom, the gypsies are demanding a harpsichord
and a box of matches. Under circumstances like these, who could
blame you if your skin sprouted azaleas, if you allowed catbirds
in the tea room, or whistled into dark places? Then comes a
resurgence of mice, one for each habit you thought you'd kicked,
or at least slapped meaningfully, but they look charming
in their little pink bow-ties that you can't help but smile,
which of course isn't allowed. Now someone is pounding on the door,
shouting "Police!"; now the locusts have come; there's a man outside
wearing a placard and pointing at the sky; you don't want to read
the placard; you've done enough reading, really; besides, it's time to
check the incubator, so you go to the refrigerator and take out
a bowl of raw meat; then you open the basement door, flip on the
light, and descend the twelve stairs; the incubator is humming, fed by
complex mechanisms, its status recorded by gauges and flashing
lights; you open the lid; tiny claws reach toward you; you toss in the
meat; there is growling, frantic movement, the sound of rending
flesh; you say "Soon, my babies"; then you close the lid, latch it, and
go back upstairs, where the surgeons with ball peen hammers and
rusty knives are waiting.

Lithuanian Holiday

The bishop is getting his miter dry-cleaned.
A wave deposits black sea glass on the shore.
A little breeze keeps changing its mind.
Every Lithuanian crow wishes it was an American mocking bird,
so that it could add to its superior intellect the talent of mimicry.
Instead, it learns how to count. But enough allegory!
A cloud shaped and colored like an eggplant persuades my cousin
to marry beneath her station. "It's for the best," we concede,
although the ceremony is followed by eight years of famine.
Meanwhile, Father assembles his space telescope.
Mother runs off with Jack o' Sundays, who's known for strangling
poets in their sleep. Does she think she can change him?
Just last week he boasted "I'll grind their beauty into a powder
for rich men's soup. I'll send their 'true love' through a jackal's
entrails, that it might fertilize the fields and spur the thistle."
This pleases Aunt Gabria, who is growing brambles for the next
crucifixion. Did I mention she once saw a white stork
in a moonlit arbor? She claims it spoke to her, mystically, but in
French, so she did not understand. Folks have called her crazy
ever since. At our last family reunion, she proposed a game of
Find-The-Fingernail, but because of the famine, we had no buckets
of rice to hide it in. And so, once more, we learned to do without.

Night Shift Narrator

After you fell asleep reading in bed, I took over as the narrator.

And then the snakes returned, I said.

And they did.

They slithered through the open door and gathered into a single, writhing current, flowing upstairs toward Isabella's bedroom.

Pleased with this effort, I added *Then the lawn caught a fever.*

And sure enough, *the grass became warm to the touch and wilted.*

The Victorian novel you'd been reading was taking on new psychological dimensions.

I felt my powers rising, so I went on.

The shadows by the tool shed began to grow fingers.

"This wall has leprosy!" Doctor Honecker exclaimed.

Judith discovered to her horror that someone—or something—had tracked phosphorous across the attic floor. "Has anyone seen my Reginald?" she cried.

Ivan was convinced that parts of the house were turning carnivorous.

Clearly the story now carried more emotional freight.

But without you being awake to experience it, most of the fun was drained away.

I watched you lying in bed with the book open on your chest, an expression of beatific calm softening your features.

You weren't a restless sleeper like so many of the other readers. No snoring or leg twitching or drooling.

Instead, you resembled a marble sculpture of a Raphael angel, perfectly serene, as though possessing secret knowledge.

I'd never known serenity. I wanted that knowledge, too, so, even though it was against the rules, I slid under the covers beside you.

I felt heat radiating from your body; it was a pleasurable sensation, so simple and wordless, and yet it was new to me.

I gently picked up the book and set it aside, then rested my head on your breast, listening to your soft, steady breathing.

"Why can't I sleep, too?" I asked myself.

But maybe I'd never tried.

And so we lay like that for a few minutes, and, lulled by your heartbeat, I swear I'd nearly drifted off, when the mold in the basement began to develop a personality.

 I could hear it *whispering beneath the floorboards—an indistinguishable murmuring at first, then swelling into something like a chant.*

"Is that Latin?" I asked myself, and I wanted to wake you and ask if you heard it, too.

But that definitely wasn't allowed, so I clasped you tighter, almost like a lover, and I didn't let go, not even when *the bedroom mirror slipped down from the wall, positioned itself beside the bed, and began to scream our names.*

Waiting for the Exterminator

I could hear them through the walls, an "uninvited choir."

Oddly-shaped welts resembling the letters of a foreign language covered my dog and me.

The little Nasties had built their nest beneath the front door. Old friends, arriving for a visit with a bottle of wine, left in pain, full of recriminations, swearing never to return.

This could not go on.

The Exterminator Headquarters promised that a representative would arrive in a beautiful white truck, though they couldn't say precisely when.

"Don't leave your house unless absolutely necessary," they told me. "Try not to establish a clear time pattern for your departures—don't let them learn your routine, or they'll lie in wait."

"Also, keep your windows closed and your shades drawn. The less they can see of you, the better."

"Try not to cook meat. That'll stir them up even more. And whatever you do, don't try to communicate with them. It won't end well."

I promised to obey their injunctions.

I drew the shades, subsisted on rice and vegetables, and tried not to speak.

I sat in my armchair, pretending to read, pretending to ignore the sound they made inside the walls. In the early days, it had seemed nothing more than murmuring—as if the house had indigestion.

But lately those indiscriminate noises had begun to congeal into patterns, with distinct pitch changes and possibly even rhythms.

My dog seemed to notice, too. He cocked his head, ran to the wall, and sniffed along the baseboard, making strange whimpering sounds, as if in response to the noises they made.

"Hey, buddy! Get away from there!" I said. "No communicating, remember?"

The dog turned to me and showed his teeth. Then he skulked over to the corner and lay down, resting his head on his paws and watching me. I could see little white crescent moons on the circumference of his eyes.

"What's wrong, pal?" I said. He showed his teeth again.

That's when I decided to forego sleep. I needed to be ready when the exterminator pulled into my driveway in his shiny, white truck— which could happen any time. And besides, I could no longer trust my dog to watch over me, now that his allegiance was compromised.

It's hard to tell how long I sat there, partly because the shades were drawn, partly because my fatigued condition blurred the boundary between hours, between night and day.

I tried to read—my library is quite extensive, and my scholarship a source of personal pride—but in my febrile state, I imagined that the words on the page were being whispered by the things inside the walls, that their narrative went on whispering even as I drifted momentarily out of consciousness, their story bearing me along the way a river bears a raft—and then I would snap awake with a jolt. I would check the words I'd been hearing against those printed on the page, and I'd find discrepancies, distinct changes in meaning--some great, some small—which led me to conclude that those Nasties were trying to seduce me with their discourse.

At the same time, my sting marks were darkening, taking on a more distinct shape, as if my skin was merely an empty page for their inscriptions.

Oh, you who still count the days, let no one deny the existence of waking dreams! The brain will have its R.E.M. state whether or not we sleep.

And what are dreams but visitations—infestations from another plane? From inside or outside—what does it matter? Such distinctions are a rationalist's mirage.

I tell you this: when the one voice disintegrates—then are we born!

We live in the membrane of your memory.

Your pain preserves us.

The white truck will never come.

Cash and Carry

Someone removed all the lids, as right reason dictated.

I offered you a rose, pressed in wax paper by Saint Rita of Cascia herself. "Thanks," you said—and tossed it in your glove box. "I hear they're serving lo mein at the race track. Wanna get some?"

Was this the cause for which we sacrificed so little?

From the far side of the mountain, I call to the dead.

The carousel operator wants to show me what's beneath his eye patch. "This same cloth once lined a magpie's nest," he tells me. "Your mother used it to cover her ring finger."

Have we been hiding evidence of ourselves in the mirror again?

Are these maxims not to your liking?

Sorry. I am the loud man of the moment. To serve the winter's austerities, my blood grows thicker. I watch the wind pull birds along a silver chain.

Someone's been ice-fishing in the golf course pond. Was it you?

You invite me over to meet your seeing-eye chimera. It's small as chimeras go, lying curled at your feet, but it watches me the whole time. Whenever I imagine you naked, which is often, it growls.

It's always cold in your apartment. "Warm your hands over the *ignis fatuus*," you tell me. "Would you like some endive?"

"Please," I say.

In your hallway, a drawbridge operator with a tapir light tells me that he's always dreamed of a life on the sea. He raises the light so I can see through his wounds. "Beware the larceny of dreams," he says. His wounds resemble the Pleiades—or is it the freckles on your back?

Can someone help me count these lids? I can no longer remember which lid goes with which container, but perhaps if I tally them, some good will come of it.

"The endive is served!" you announce, resplendent in your nakedness.

The chimera bares its teeth. It makes as if to lunge. But what can it do to me—a remembered thing, a voice and a shadow, like itself?

Night of the Multivalent Cupids

A dyslexic light settles over the cul de sac.
Something has roused the suburbanites;
maybe it's that new song kids are humming;
maybe it's oxytocin; maybe it's those spoors
wafting above the limestone quarries—
"you gotta squint to see 'em, and even then
it's hard to know what you're looking at."

Suddenly everyone's a narrator.
Uncle Theron wants to know
"Is skinny-dipping still a 'thing'? Wax lips?
Who do you think planned the high school dance?
Why is nougat a good idea?"
I can list my compunctions alphabetically,
but that doesn't mean I'm no longer smitten
—after all, it's the gong no one strikes that gets you!

Meanwhile, it may help to focus on a few particulars:
creek beds littered with discarded cummerbunds;
fruit-flavored cigars; pushups by moonlight;
binomials waiting to be multiplied; the gritty bon mots
you brought up with the latest Heimlich maneuver.
The Bells of Saint Anthony's couldn't put it any plainer:
your loneliness explains your promiscuity.

Of course, those bells were stolen long ago.
Now something's buzzing near the acacias.
The spoors have molted into paradigms,
and the fragile line between cleanliness and Godliness

threatens to resolve itself into a dew.
And there you are, curled up like a cowslip in a coal-miner's dream.

But hey, this moon-blight becomes you,
the fat boys are yodeling, and all the weathervanes are looking up.
It's a night for false consciousness and minstrelsy-by-numbers,
so why not roll all our strife into one gray futon
before your parents get home? Then we can light
some sparklers and feast on sloppy joes as if nothing happened.
Come to think of it, maybe it did.

Future Pastoral

The stream will cease its flute music. What butterflies are left will take a dirigible to work.

The periodic tables will have to be revised—or discarded, like a magician's cards that have lost their magic due to the hole in the ozone.

The alchemists will make a comeback.

"What is it we are herding?" the shepherds ask, finding themselves in three piece suits. "Should we still sing of love? What is love? What is singing?"

Lava carves the heath into a smoldering chessboard.

The alchemists prospect for lead amidst the skeleton heaps. Silver fillings in the skulls' teeth pick up radio signals from fifty years ago. The more cavities, the better the reception...

A sphinx emerges from a crack in the earth, arms bristling with new algebraic equations. The equations bleed and whimper. Jack Horner develops a rash while hunting wood sprites, using the eyelids and tonsils of children as bait.

And the moon signals the stars to let go their bitter albumen.

Pastoral, With High Pollen Count

Another morning's casuistry left its tracings in the mud.
Not coincidently, I found your shed skin on the front porch step, all
dewy and translucent. A sound like Daddy chewing Corn Flakes
arose from the orchards. Had summer run its course so soon?

Ah, summer, with its umlauts and flaxen hair, its many zippers!
What had become of those nighttime rides along the Baltic,
with the moon-roof cracked open like a dental patient's jaw,
and all those tree frogs singing Agnus Dei? Was it only yesterday

we itched like crazy? Watching your skin under the changing light
fueled my nostalgia—how could it not? Remember those mosquitos
whispering Scheherazade in our ears? They were as big as
the nose on your face; we prayed they'd bite in the right places!

And then, as I reminisced, the satyrs crept out of the storm drain,
sprinkled costume jewelry under the eaves. My dog rolled in
something. Soon the sun was squatting on its haunches. I took off all
my clothes, watched a tide of Queen Ann's lace roll across the yard.

I remained affixed to my lawn chair; hallucinatory flute music wafted
in the breeze. Another ransom note arrived by carrier pigeon.
The sundial cleared its throat. By late afternoon your skin had turned
        papery, even brittle.
At last I could give you the affection we both deserved.

More poetry published by SurVision Books

Noelle Kocot. *Humanity*
(New Poetics: USA)
ISBN 978-1-9995903-0-7

Ciaran O'Driscoll. *The Speaking Trees*
(New Poetics: Ireland)
ISBN 978-1-9995903-1-4

Helen Ivory. *Maps of the Abandoned City*
(New Poetics: England)
ISBN 978-1-912963-04-1

Elin O'Hara Slavick. *Cameramouth*
(New Poetics: USA)
ISBN 978-1-9995903-4-5

John W. Sexton. *Inverted Night*
(New Poetics: Ireland)
ISBN 978-1-912963-05-8

Afric McGlinchey. *Invisible Insane*
(New Poetics: Ireland)
ISBN 978-1-9995903-3-8

Anatoly Kudryavitsky. *Stowaway*
(New Poetics: Ireland)
ISBN 978-1-9995903-2-1

Tim Murphy. *The Cacti Do Not Move*
(New Poetics: Ireland)
ISBN 978-1-912963-07-2

Tony Kitt. *The Magic Phlute*
(New Poetics: Ireland)
ISBN 978-1-912963-08-9

Clayre Benzadón. *Liminal Zenith*
(New Poetics: USA)
ISBN 978-1-912963-11-9

George Kalamaras. *That Moment of Wept*
ISBN 978-1-9995903-7-6

Anton Yakovlev. *Chronos Dines Alone*
(Winner of James Tate Poetry Prize 2018)
ISBN 978-1-912963-01-0

Bob Lucky. *Conversation Starters in a Language No One Speaks*
(Winner of James Tate Poetry Prize 2018)
ISBN 978-1-912963-00-3

Christopher Prewitt. *Paradise Hammer*
(Winner of James Tate Poetry Prize 2018)
ISBN 978-1-9995903-9-0

Mikko Harvey & Jake Bauer. *Idaho Falls*
(Winner of James Tate Poetry Prize 2018)
ISBN 978-1-912963-02-7

Tony Bailie. *Mountain Under Heaven*
(Winner of James Tate Poetry Prize 2019)
ISBN 978-1-912963-09-6

Nicholas Alexander Hayes. *Amorphous Organics*
(Winner of James Tate Poetry Prize 2019)
ISBN 978-1-912963-10-2

John Bradley. *Spontaneous Mummification*
(Winner of James Tate Poetry Prize 2019)
ISBN 978-1-912963-13-3

Gary Glauber. *The Covalence of Equanimity*
(Winner of James Tate Poetry Prize 2019)
ISBN 978-1-912963-12-6

Maria Grazia Calandrone. *Fossils*
Translated from Italian
(New Poetics: Italy)
ISBN 978-1-9995903-6-9

Sergey Biryukov. *Transformations*
Translated from Russian
(New Poetics: Russia)
ISBN 978-1-9995903-5-2

Alexander Korotko. *Irrazionalismo*
Translated from Russian
(New Poetics: Ukraine)
ISBN 978-1-912963-06-5

Anton G. Leitner. *Selected Poems 1981–2015*
Translated from German
ISBN 978-1-9995903-8-3

All our books are available to order via
http://survisionmagazine.com/books.htm

Made in United States
North Haven, CT
14 March 2023

34045053R00024